NATIONAL THEATRE PLAYS

THE FORCE OF HABIT

THE FORCE OF HABIT

A Comedy
by

THOMAS BERNHARD

Translated by
Neville and Stephen Plaice

'I myself wavered as a young man between comedy
and the Sorbonne'
—Diderot

'. . . but the race of prophets has become
extinct . . .'
—Artaud

HEINEMANN
in association with the National Theatre
LONDON

Heinemann Educational Books Ltd
LONDON EDINBURGH MELBOURNE TORONTO
JOHANNESBURG NEW DELHI AUCKLAND
SINGAPORE HONG KONG NAIROBI
IBADAN KUALA LUMPUR KINGSTON

ISBN
0 435 23120 0

© Thomas Bernhard 1974
© English translation Neville & Stephen Plaice 1976

First published 1976

All rights whatsoever in this play are strictly reserved and on no account may performances be given unless written permission has been obtained.

Applications must be made in advance to:
Rosica Colin Ltd
7 Hereford Square, London SW7 4TU

Published by
Heinemann Educational Books Ltd
48 Charles Street, London W1X 8AH
Set in 10/11pt Garamond by
Spectrum Typesetting, London
and printed in Great Britain by
Biddles of Guildford

INTRODUCTION

by

Neville and Stephen Plaice

Thomas Bernhard

Thomas Bernhard was born in Heerlen in Holland in 1931 of Austrian parents and he has spent most of his life in Austria. He had musical training as a boy and eventually went on to study music and drama in Vienna. As well as intermittently producing literary and musical work in the 1950s, he worked for a time as a newspaper reporter and also travelled extensively in Europe. His first important work, the novel *Frost*, was published in 1963. Since then he has maintained a prolific output of prose. He regards his novels as his major work. In 1968 he was awarded the Austrian State Prize for his prose, and in 1970, one of Germany's most valued distinctions, the Büchner Prize. His first full-length play was staged in Hamburg in the same year—*A Party for Boris*. He was quickly recognised as one of the major innovators in dramatic form writing in German. The very format of his plays distinguishes him from other dramatists. The way he breaks up the sentences on the page exposes the habits of language, rendering it unfamiliar. Two of his plays have had premières at the Salzburg Festival, *The Ignoramus and The Madman* in 1972, and *The Force of Habit* in 1974. Since 1965 he has lived on a remote farm in Ohlsdorf in the Upper Austrian Alps, a landscape that often appears in his works and which also inspired Schubert to write *The Trout Quintet*, the piece of music central to *The Force of Habit*.

The Force of Habit

The play forces together two radically different spheres of art, the circus on the one hand, and the performance of classical music on the other. A ringmaster attempts to perfect Schubert's quintet with the four other members of his troupe. Yet this is not just a comedy that plays off the circus against serious musicianship, character deficiencies against the impossible ideal of a perfect art, or Caribaldi against his troupe. There is another associated struggle that holds the stage, the internal struggle of the characters to emerge from the purely habitual and private gestures of their language. To illustrate the force of linguistic habit, Bernhard has borrowed the musical idea of 'theme and variations' from the fourth movement of the Trout Quintet and has applied it to the language of a play. The characters' words and themes recur automatically, not only in their own, but also in each other's mouths, sometimes with minor variations, but often for the mere reassurance of naming things over and over again. Like their instruments, the characters must not let go of their theme for too long. They must always have a store of words to fall back on when their attempts at breaking new ground fail.

Bernhard takes the theme of habit into areas usually associated with the extraordinary and the spectacular. But behind artistry, whether circus or classical music, there must be rehearsal. The performers become what they rehearse. Here, even their voices seem to take on the same tone as their instruments. They can escape neither their circus nor their musical roles. Caribaldi is no exception. For him the perfecting of the Trout Quintet means escape from the arbitrariness of the world. Yet, even though he knows it is impossible, given the defective characters of his troupe, he continues the gesture of rehearsal. He has been rehearsing the quintet so long, it too has become a habit of mind. The escape from habit through art is merely turned into another layer of habit.

The comedy, however, relies just as heavily on rehearsal, on timing and virtuosity, so that it is itself open to the fun it pokes at Caribaldi's hopeless mixture of circus and the Trout Quintet. That mixture, curiously, is also the author's. Like the ringmaster, Bernhard has to balance the two arts, only in his case he also has to extract a third art from them, the comedy. He too struggles to perfect. He too has to make a ruthless habit of precision. So he himself is open to the laughter he creates at the expense of his characters. That is another variation on the theme of the force of habit. Not even Thomas Bernhard or his play can escape it.

* * * * *

All Bernhard's work is concerned with the themes of isolation and decay. When he was awarded the State Prize, he accepted with the words, 'Everything is ridiculous when one thinks of death', at which point the Minister of Education stormed out of the hall. But Bernhard was not being morbid. He sees death as an ever-present, creative force in existence, not something alien at the end of it. In the words of Caribaldi, 'Durch den Tod wird das Leben verstärkt' (Life is intensified by means of death). Decay has always been a major theme of Austrian writing.

Bernhard recently explained why:

Here you find every possible sickness in its most extreme form. You can find it expressed every day in the newspapers and in the faces of the people who read them or don't read them. The country is ruled by madmen and fools—but madmen and fools who are, on the whole, lovable and sympathetic. It's the result of history, naturally, as everything is—but the fact remains, everyone behaves as though they were sick and mad. Don't think I've escaped all this. Not at all. I too am sick and mad. It is an Austrian characteristic. The Germans have too little sense of humour to be really mad. They are too serious. They have too much of the schoolmaster about them; they're too primitive; at too low a spiritual level to be really sick and mad. The Austrians are not too primitive, so they can be sick and mad. For that, there has to be a certain greatness.*

The affinity between disease, madness and artistic creation holds a central place in the German philosophical tradition, culminating in the works of Schopenhauer and Nietzsche. There are many echoes of their ideas in the rambling, disjointed monologues of Caribaldi. But, ironically, Bernhard himself, with his insistence on the fundamental relationship between art and death, is clearly writing from within the same tradition that he is parodying in *The Force of Habit*.

*BBC interview given to Charles Marowitz.

The Trout Quintet

In July 1819, accompanied by his friend Vogl, Franz Schubert went on holiday to Upper Austria. Their first stop was at Steyr (not far from where Thomas Bernhard now lives). The composer was in light-hearted mood and was delighted by his surroundings. 'The country around Steyr is inconceivably lovely,' he wrote to his brother. Through his friend, he was introduced to the amateur musicians of the town and received much attention from their wives and daughters on account of his musical ability. 'At the house where I lodge there are eight girls, nearly all pretty. Plenty to do, you see,' he wrote. In this pleasant atmosphere Schubert composed the Trout Quintet, so called because its fourth movement, the theme and variations, was based on his song 'The Trout', written two years earlier, and because it attempted to suggest the leaping of trout in an alpine stream. It is probable that the piece was written for the amateurs in Steyr, and that the unusual combination of instruments employed in the quintet reflected their capabilities rather than Schubert's own choice. It may even have been commissioned by the amateurs. The critics are in no doubt that the music was merely a piece of holiday entertainment written to capture the buoyant mood of the company and of the mountains in summer. For instance, J.A. Westrup writes: It is entertainment music from first to last and should be listened to with simple unsophisticated enjoyment. To drink—even to talk—during a performance would not be blasphemy.

N. & S. Plaice

CAST OF FIRST LONDON PRODUCTION

The **Force of Habit** was first presented by the National Theatre Company at the Lyttleton Theatre, London in November 1976. The company was as follows:

Caribaldi, ringmaster	Philip Locke
Granddaughter	Brenda Blethyn
Juggler	Gawn Grainger
Lion-Tamer	Warren Clarke
Clown	Oliver Cotton
Director	Elijah Moshinsky
Designers	Timothy O'Brien
	Tazeena Firth
Lighting	David Hersey
Movement	Eleanor Fazan
Staff Director	Michael Turner
Production Manager	Martin McCallum
Stage Manager	Jennifer Smith
Deputy Stage Managers	Elizabeth Markham
	Robin Miskimmin
Assistant Stage Managers	Douglas Attrill
	Francesca Bailey
	Jondon Gourkan
Sound	Chris Montgomery

CHARACTERS

Caribaldi, ringmaster
Granddaughter
Juggler
Lion-Tamer
Clown

Scene: CARIBALDI'S CARAVAN

SCENE ONE

Caribaldi's *caravan.*
A piano stage left. Four music-stands in the foreground. Chest, table with radio, armchair, mirror, pictures. The Trout quintet on the floor.
Caribaldi *looking for something under the chest.* **Juggler** *comes in.*

Juggler: What are you doing there
　The quintet is on the floor
　Mr Caribaldi
　Augsburg tomorrow
　isn't it
Caribaldi: Augsburg tomorrow
Juggler: The lovely quintet
　　Picks up the quintet.
　By the way
　I got the letter from France
　　Puts the quintet on one of the music-stands.
　Just imagine
　a guaranteed sum
　But experience shows
　that an offer
　ought not to be accepted
　straight away
　That's what experience shows
　　Arranges the quintet on the music-stand.
　In Bordeaux above all
　the white wine

What are you looking for down there
Mr Caribaldi
  Takes the cello that is leaning on the chair, dusts it with his right sleeve and leans it on the chair again.
Covered in dust
everything covered in dust
Because we are playing
on such a dusty site
It is windy here
and dusty
Caribaldi: Augsburg tomorrow
Juggler: Augsburg tomorrow
Why are we playing here
I ask myself
Why ask
That is your business
Mr Caribaldi
Caribaldi: Augsburg tomorrow
Juggler: Augsburg tomorrow
of course
To leave the cello
out of its case
even for only a few moments
  Blows dust off the cello.
Negligence
Mr Caribaldi
  Picks up the cello.
The Maggini
isn't it
No
the Salo
the so-called
Ferraracello
  Leans the cello on the chair again and takes a step back, inspecting the cello.
A musical
treasure
But of course
we cannot only

play
on asphalt-covered sites
North of the Alps
the Salo
the Ferraracello
south of the Alps
the Maggini
or
before five o'clock in the afternoon
the Maggini
and after five o'clock in the afternoon
the Ferraracello
the Salo
  Dusts the cello.
A dying profession
  Suddenly to **Caribaldi**.
What are you looking for
Caribaldi: The rosin
Juggler: The rosin
  Of course
  The rosin
  Time after time the rosin
  Because the fingers suffer from the weakness
  notorious among instrumentalists
  Haven't you got
  a second
  a so-called
  rosin reserve
  As a child
  You know I played
  the violin
  as a child
  I had two emerald-green boxes
  in each of these emerald-green boxes
  I had a rosin reserve
  What it comes down to
  always
  in reserve
  you know

> One must
> if one is a practising instrumentalist
> have rosin in reserve

Caribaldi: In Augsburg tomorrow

Juggler: In Augsburg tomorrow
> Mr Caribaldi

Caribaldi: It must be there
> under the chest

Juggler *(bends down and also looks under the chest)*:
> I am expected
> in Bordeaux
> a five-year contract
> Mr Caribaldi
> What's more my act with the plates has
> a decidedly French appeal
> Six on the left
> eight on the right
> little by little
> set to music
> you know
> And clothes allowance
> extra
> a new suit
> Mr Caribaldi
> Parisian velvet
> Parisian silk
> By Alexandre
> you know
> an elegant lining
>> *Suddenly.*
> But look
> there
> is the rosin
>> *Stands up.*

Caribaldi: There it is
> *Fetches the rosin out from under the chest.*

Juggler: You should buy yourself a second box
> in Augsburg

Caribaldi: In Augsburg tomorrow

Juggler: I am expected
in Bordeaux
Sarrasani
that is always
a triumph
the highest class
Mr Caribaldi
and from Bordeaux
right down
to Portugal
Lisbon
Oporto
you know
    Caribaldi goes to the cello with the rosin, sits down and rubs the bow with the rosin.
For a juggler
who has no command
of the French language
not the easiest thing
but I do have a command of
the French language
French was the mother tongue
of my mother
Pablo Casals always had
five or six pieces of rosin
in reserve
In Augsburg tomorrow
Caribaldi: In Augsburg tomorrow
Juggler: What's more
This extraordinary woman
my mother
left the Church in Nantes
Caribaldi *(rubbing the cello bow evenly with the rosin)*:
The rosin
is always falling
from my hand
on to the floor
Juggler: Weak fingers
Mr Caribaldi

      possibly
      due to old age
Caribaldi: A second box of rosin
Juggler: For years I have been saying
    buy yourself
    a second box of rosin
Caribaldi: In Augsburg tomorrow
Juggler: Under the chest
      Points under the chest.
    Over there
        Juggler *and* **Caribaldi** *look under the chest.*
    Always under the chest
    down there
    but that is very interesting
    Weak fingers
    and the law of gravity
Caribaldi: For one or two years
    I have only been able to hold the rosin
    in my hand with difficulty
Juggler: Your hand
    is used to the whip
    not to the rosin
    Mr Caribaldi
      Caribaldi *opens his dirty waistcoat.* **Juggler** *jumps up and rushes over to a picture hanging crooked on the wall and straightens it, a second one as well, and sits down again.*
Juggler: All day I have been thinking
    how long have you been practising the quintet
    fifteen
    or maybe twenty years
    as long as I can remember
    from the first day
    I joined up with you
    I remember
    you have been sitting here on the chair
    rehearsing the Trout quintet
Caribaldi: I've been practising
    the Trout quintet
    for twenty years

>   twenty two years
>   to be precise
>   A therapy
>   you know
>   Play an instrument
>   a string-instrument
>   my doctor said
>   to keep your concentration from flagging

Juggler: For you were afraid of nothing so much
>   as the flagging of your concentration

Caribaldi: Concentration
>   must not be allowed to flag
>   At that time
>   twenty-two years ago
>   my concentration had
>   suddenly flagged
>   With the crack of the whip
>   no precision
>   you see
>   no precision
>   with the crack of the whip

Juggler: The horses didn't react any more

Caribaldi: Not precisely
>   not with the
>   necessary precision
>   And now I have been playing
>   or rather practising
>   the cello for twenty-two years

Juggler: And for twenty-two years
>   the Trout quintet

>   **Caribaldi** *holds the lowest note for a long time.*

Juggler: An artist
>   who practises an art
>   needs another second art
>   the one art
>   from the other
>   the one set of skills
>   from the other

>   **Caribaldi** *stretches out his right hand to* **Juggler**.

Caribaldi: The whole trouble
is in this hand
you see
I drop the rosin
> *Withdraws his hand.*
And my head
is no longer able
to concentrate
suddenly
concentration flags
The love of performance alone
Juggler: Certainly
Art
is nothing but reciprocal action
performance
art
art
performance
you see
I wonder whether
the rehearsal will take place today
Your granddaughter
is unwell
the clown
is depressed
and today the lion-tamer
is yet again a prey
to his melancholy
This is a term
Mr Caribaldi
a medical term
Caribaldi: The last rehearsal
was a disgrace
I do not want to go through that
again
> *Holds the lowest note for a long time.*
A drunken lion-tamer
who has difficulty standing up
a clown whose cap

    is continually falling from his head
    a granddaughter who by virtue of her very existence
    gets on my nerves
    The truth is a debacle
Juggler: Wednesday is always
    a bad day
    But Saturday isn't
    a good day either
    Even the animals are different on Wednesday
    than on Saturday
    different on Saturday
    than on Wednesday
    But from people
    especially performers
    artists
    Mr Caribaldi
    we can surely expect
    self-control
Caribaldi: If we succeeded just once
    just one single time
    in completing
    the Trout quintet
    one single time perfect music
Juggler: A work of art
    Mr Caribaldi
Caribaldi: To make this practice
    into art
Juggler: Without a hitch
    such a lovely piece
Caribaldi: Such a great work of art
    you know
    In these twenty-two years
    we haven't succeeded one single time
    in completing
    the Trout quintet
    without making a mistake
    let alone making a work of art
    There is always someone
    who ruins everything

      through carelessness
      or vulgarity
Juggler: Inability to concentrate
    Mr Caribaldi
Caribaldi: First it is the violin
    then it is the viola
    then it is the bass
    then it is the piano
    Then again I get
    this deadly back-ache
    I am doubled up in pain
    you know
    and the piece of music falls apart
    When I get the clown
    to master his instrument
    the lion-tamer loses his head
    on the piano
    or my granddaughter
    who has been playing the viola
    for at least ten years
    gets a splinter
    in her hand
    like last Tuesday
    You can't play Schubert
    with a face distorted by pain
    especially not the Trout quintet
    I was not to know
    it is so difficult
    to serve the art of music
      Holds a note on the cello.
    And I can't play the quintet
    on my own
    It is a quintet
    Rubs the bow again with rosin while the **Juggler** *is speaking.*
Juggler: The great loyalty I feel
    on the one hand
    Bordeaux
    France Mr Caribaldi

on the other
Clothes extra
you see
and
up and down the Riviera
all winter
and the chance
of working together with my sister
    Caribaldi *drops the rosin, the* **Juggler** *picks it up.*
It will be completely different
in France
Mr Caribaldi
A dream
come true
As you know
I am exceptionally fond
of eating fresh mussels
in white Bordeaux
on the Atlantic coast
    Gives **Caribaldi** *the rosin.*
The German language
stultifies as time goes on
the German language
clamps down on your head
    Grasps his head in his hands, **Caribaldi** *plucks the cello,*
Juggler *watching* **Caribaldi**
Clothes bonus extra
And French fresh air
Mr Caribaldi
    Caribaldi *plays a long low note on the cello.* **Juggler** *watching* **Caribaldi** *even more closely.*
This posture
of the upper part of the body
was attained by Casals
at his peak
    Caribaldi *plucks the cello.*
The constant change of air
now north
now south of the Alps

harms the instrument
It must constantly be re-tuned
and always according to different factors
for each new place
for each new atmosphere extra
Caribaldi: Extra
Juggler: But so-called chamber music
is in your family
in my family too
    Caribaldi *plays a low note on the cello.*
And it is always
the Trout quintet
Best you say yourself
in Prague
worst of all
on the Theresienwiese
Caribaldi: Augsburg tomorrow
Juggler: On the Theresienwiese
    Caribaldi *plays a low note, plucks the cello.*
Art is a means
for another art
    Thoughtfully
It is always
the last performance
The tent is already being dismantled
even during my act with the plates
    Looks and points upwards.
Because I have to look up
I see
the tent being dismantled
The audience of course does not
notice it
    Caribaldi *plucks the cello.*
The concentration of the audience
is focused on me
    Goes and straightens pictures and mirror.
An advantage
to have a French mother
As you know

my father is from Gelsenkirchen
an unfortunate man
he was engaged for a while
in ship-building
> *Suddenly.*

I am stopping at eighteen
Eighteen plates no more
I was suddenly afraid
Mr Caribaldi
> *Looks at* **Caribaldi**'s *waistcoat.*

Your waistcoat is dirty
Mr Caribaldi
> **Caribaldi** *plays a low note on the cello.*

Your waistcoat is dirty
Mr Caribaldi

Caribaldi: Crawling about
on the floor all day
looking
for the rosin
> *Takes the rosin and rubs the bow of the cello, as the* **Juggler**
says

Juggler: I have been offered
a one-man show
for a whole evening
at the sanatorium in Rouen
you see
The act with the poodle
on top of my act with the plates
The artificial poodle

Caribaldi: Your act with the artificial poodle

Juggler: This artificial poodle act
which you have forbidden me
Two years sacrificed to this act
and then you banned it
I can do this act in Rouen
And my sister is accepted
as an assistant
Sarrasani
Mr Caribaldi

The phrase is your own phrase
Move on
don't stand still
don't stand still
move on
   Exclaims.
I am going to France
Mr Caribaldi
   Caribaldi *plucks the cello.*
Caribaldi: Augsburg tomorrow
Juggler: Augsburg tomorrow
   Straightens a picture.
Sarrasani
Mr Caribaldi
   Caribaldi *plays a low note on the cello.*
In reality
it is not my act with the plates at all
it isn't me either
it is the violin
Mr Caribaldi
It is the Trout quintet
that is nothing without me
You have forced me
   Caribaldi *plucks the cello.*
to play the violin
because in an unhappy moment
I gave myself away
and said
that I played the violin as a child
You forced me back to the violin
with incredible ruthlessness
   Caribaldi *plays a low note on the cello.*
And you forced the viola
on your granddaughter
And the bass on the clown
And the piano
on your nephew the lion-tamer
   Shouts.
Forced

forced
> *Sets a mirror straight as if to compose himself.*

Besides which your nephew
hates playing the piano
> *Suddenly pointing at the door.*

Through this door
your victims enter
Mr Caribaldi
your instruments
Mr Caribaldi
Not people
Instruments
> *Pointing at the piano.*

Your nephew the lion-tamer
once had the idea
of smashing the piano
with an axe
he did not do it
although the axe was already raised
I prevented it
You know the brutality of your nephew
as you say yourself
The animal
If you don't
I do
Perhaps a so-called fit
but the very thought
of the smashed piano
and just think
of the piano
smashed by your nephew
your own flesh and blood
my head aches
my head aches
> *Grasps his head in his hands and moans.*

I took the axe away
from your nephew
On that occasion
I handled your nephew

as your nephew
handles his so-called wild animals
I went up to him
> **Caribaldi** *plays a low note on the cello.*

I used friendly persuasion
I soothed him
Then I promised him
> **Caribaldi** *looks up.*

that I would disclose to him the secret
of my artificial poodle act
Like this
> *He demonstrates.*

your nephew had the axe above his head
how easy for him
to smash
the piano with a single blow
You know his strength
You know his strength of purpose
> *Takes a music-stand and blows off the dust.* **Caribaldi** *plays a long low note on the cello.*

But I could not keep
my promise
Because you threatened me with the sack
if I explained to your nephew
the trick
or rather the art
of the artificial poodle act
I was dependent on your help
the act with the plates was not yet
developed to the extent
that I could have made myself independent
I could not
punch you in the face
I could not afford to do that
I could not blackmail you
You blackmailed me
I was at your mercy again
My nephew plays
the piano

as long as I say he does
you said
   Points to the corner.
Over there in the corner
you said that
That was final
   Picks up a music-book and blows off the dust.
You dominate your nephew
like your granddaughter
The clown only clowns about
Because you force him to
All these people
are at your mercy
If these people dare for once
not to come
not to play
the Trout quintet
But they do not dare commit
such an atrocity
   Caribaldi *plucks the cello.*
These people
are at your mercy
possess nothing
and are at your mercy
Even I have never had the courage
not to play
   Sits down.
On the contrary
I encouraged them to play
   Grasps his head in his hands.
This head's to blame
for such inconsistency
consistency
Your term
precision
consistency
these two
your terms
But of course you suffer too

17

in this typical
megalomaniac approach of yours
from your own ruthlessness
Mr Caribaldi
And the causes
are your back-ache
and your wooden leg
Caribaldi: Augsburg tomorrow
Juggler: Your health already impaired
from childhood on
Your hypersensitiveness
below the scalp
Mr Caribaldi
Suddenly vehement.
The invalid and the cripple
rule the world
everything is ruled by the sick
and by the deformed
It's a farce
a wicked humiliation
Caribaldi plays a low note on the cello.
If like me one serves
a genius I grant you
for over a decade
and everything
Caribaldi bursts out laughing.
And everything is rewarded
with laughter
Produces a letter from his coat pocket.
But now
I have this letter
from France
The ringmaster Sarrasani himself
has written to me
Caribaldi stops laughing. **Juggler** *purposefully with the letter above his head.*
Anyone who receives
such an offer in his life
who

Caribaldi *makes four short passes on the cello, thrusts it from him without letting go of it.*
Caribaldi *(peremptory)*:
The Maggini
no
The Salo;
The Ferraracello
Don't you understand
I want the Ferraracello
    Juggler *takes the cello from him.* **Caribaldi** *commanding.*
The Ferraracello
    Juggler *over to the chest with the Maggini cello, takes out the so-called Ferraracello and puts the Maggini cello inside.*
Perfection
Perfection
you see
nothing else
    Juggler *gives* **Caribaldi** *the so-called Ferraracello.*
My nephew
My granddaughter
what people
And Pablo Casals
What a man
    Exclaims.
What people
what creatures
what madness
every one a wretched person
in his own right
Mister Clown
how absurd
little Miss granddaughter
All these people
related or not
have cost me nothing but money
Money
and patience
A lifelong trial of nerves
Plays a low note on the cello.

Casals
he's the man
> *Rubs the bow with the rosin.*

when I see my nephew the lion-tamer
I think
there goes brutality with stupidity
when I see the clown
there's an imbecile out for a walk
imbecility
loses his hat
when I see my granddaughter
it is the vileness of her mother
Give it here
> *Tears the cello out of the* **Juggler**'s *hand, who had held it for a moment so that* **Caribaldi** *did not let it fall to the floor.*

Imbecility
Yes
Casals
or Schopenhauer
you understand
or Plato
> *Plays a long low note.*

I once dreamed
I was in Archangel
without knowing
what Archangel is like
And I know nothing but Archangel
that's it
that's all
you see
And then you think
you can just clear off
> *Exclaims.*

Sarrasani
what is that
You do your act with the plates
here in my troupe
here in this ring
perfect your art

what do I mean perfection
improve
you understand
nothing else
Make your rehearsal
into an example
you understand
Everything here is sordid
    Plays a long note on the cello.
Listen
completely different
completely different
listen
The Salo
has a completely different tone
to the Maggini
How late is it then
Do not tell me
how late it is
    Plays a long low note on the cello.
The Salo
The Ferraracello
The one before five
the other after five
    Makes five short strokes back and forth.
The Salo
listen
The humidity
north of the Alps
    Plays a low note on the cello.
You must listen very closely
a completely different tone
But if I play the Ferraracello
in the morning
it has a devastating effect
You must get that into your head
I always say to myself
the one in the morning
the other in the afternoon

Like Casals
   Thoughtfully.
Augsburg tomorrow
Juggler: Two boxes of rosin
   Mr Caribaldi
Caribaldi: But if one thinks all the time as I think
   it is madness
   The one cello in the morning
   the other in the afternoon
   you see
   The same also goes for the violin
   And for the viola too
      Plays a few brief notes on the cello. **Juggler** *fetches a violin-case from the chest and a violin from the violin-case and sits down and tunes the violin.*
Caribaldi: It has never happened to me yet
   morning rehearsal
   on the Ferraracello
   never before
   And south of the Alps
   exactly the opposite
   My granddaughter's talent
   is no great talent
   but it is graceful
   she dances on the tight-rope
   gracefully
   she plays the viola
   gracefully
   A child
   And my nephew
   a decided anti-talent
   On the other hand piano-playing is
   appropriate
   for a lion-tamer
   His relationship with animals you know
   is reversed
   These continual injuries
   In Augsburg tomorrow
   he must consult a doctor

in Augsburg tomorrow
In truth my nephew ought
to have become
what he is
a bourgeois person
through and through
I forced him
into the troupe
Juggler: The fatal bites
sustained by his predecessor
Caribaldi: Those fatal bites
Juggler: Leopard bites
Caribaldi: We had
to shoot
the leopards
That poor man
torn to pieces by the leopard
   Plays a long low note on the cello.
The quintet
seemed lost
Then it occurred to me
my nephew
Juggler: To make your nephew
a lion-tamer
and hence a pianist
Caribaldi: We had a lion-tamer
and pianist
Juggler: The quintet was saved
Caribaldi: The quintet
was saved
   Plays a long low note on the cello.
Besides it wasn't just that one time
my nephew had the idea
of smashing the piano
He has tried to do it
again and again
Juggler: By unsuitable means
of course
Caribaldi: Of course

And don't you believe the hypocrisy
of the clown
he hates the bass
My granddaughter does not like the viola either
Admit you yourself
only play the violin
on sufferance
Everything only on sufferance
everything that happens
happens on sufferance
Life existence
on sufferance
The fact is
 Juggler *goes up to a picture and straightens it.*
The fact is
I don't like the cello
It is torture for me
but it must be played
my granddaughter does not like the viola
but it must be played
the clown does not like the bass
but it must be played
the lion-tamer does not like the piano
but it must be played
And you don't like the violin either
We do not want life
but it must be lived
 Plucks the cello.
We hate the Trout quintet
but it must be played
 Juggler *sits down, takes the violin, plays it.* **Caribaldi** *plays a few notes on the cello.*
No pretending
no self-deception
 Four short notes on the cello.
What can here readily
be called a musical art
is in reality
a disease

Give me the rosin
> **Juggler** *gives* **Caribaldi** *the rosin.* **Caribaldi** *rubs the bow of the cello with the rosin.*

Casals
> *After a pause.*

Ridiculous
Art
is always
another art
the artist
or better
the conjurer
there are only conjurers
another person
every day
day in day out
another person
Above all
such a man must not
lose his self-control
His characteristic lucidity
conversant
with his madness
If he is intelligence
itself
Everything instinctive
ought to be transformed
into an act of will
The thinking organs
are the genitals of nature
and procreate the world
Everything rests on
partial harmonies
> *Plucks at the strings of the cello.*

this is not a question
of theosophy
you see
> *Plucks at the strings.*

But the madness of these people

is another kind of madness
the same with their disdain
lucidity on the one hand
disdain on the other
Penchant for disease
Overcoming life
Mortal fear
you understand
> *His ear to the cello.*

Listen
that's how Casals does it
> *Plays a long low note on the cello.*

That's how Casals does it
Always the inclination to lewdness
when it comes to the head
In a world
of intolerance
> *Plays a low note on the cello.*

Every word
is a magic word
> *Emphatically.*

Summon a ghost
and it appears
> *Drops the rosin, it rolls under the chest, throws up his right hand and cries*

These fingers
these fingers are driving me mad
> *Looking at the* **Juggler**.

That fine suit
that good cut
that tone inspiring confidence
> **Juggler** *gets down on the floor, looking for the rosin.*

How we switch our intelligence
to any channel we choose
Magical astronomy
Grammar
Philosophy
Religion
Chemistry and so on

Notion of contagion
Sympathy of the sign
with the signified
The rosin has probably
rolled right up against the wall
right up against the wall
right up against the wall

Plucks the cello. **Juggler** *looking back at* **Caribaldi** *as he searches for the rosin with his hands under the chest.*

Every arbitrary
random
trivial thing
seems to create a whole system of relationships

Puts his ear to the cello and at the same time plays a long low note.

That's it
like Casals
It is a nervous habit
a nervous disease
believe me
The rosin
insanity
you see

Throws up his right hand and nervously twitches all his fingers in the air and cries

It happens all of a sudden
all of a sudden
a disorder
a nervous disorder

After a pause

A habit
And you see

Points under the chest.

Always in that direction
always under the chest

Juggler: Collective insanity
Mr Caribaldi

Caribaldi: I have been recommended
to tie it

to a cord
and hang it round my neck
>   *Plays a long low note on the cello.*

Like mittens
you understand
round your neck
as a child

>   **Granddaughter** *enters with a basin of hot water and a towel;* **Caribaldi** *gazes at his* **Granddaughter**.

Ah yes my foot-bath
Come here my child
Juggler: Your foot-bath
Mr Caribaldi

>   **Granddaughter** *places the basin in front of* **Caribaldi** *and takes his shoes and stockings off and rolls up the bottom of his trousers to reveal his right leg is a wooden leg.* **Caribaldi** *puts his left leg in the basin of water.*

Caribaldi: Ah
Suddenly.
Where have we got to in the performance
What were the last lot of animals
the apes
Granddaughter: The apes
Caribaldi: The apes
the apes
>   *About the* **Juggler** *to the* **Granddaughter**.

He is looking for the rosin
Did you dance gracefully
faultlessly
faultlessly and gracefully
>   **Granddaughter** *nods.*

There is nothing
better than a hot
foot-bath
When the water
is just as hot
as you can
bear it
>   *Kisses his* **Granddaughter** *on the brow, she steps back,*

suddenly.
But you are freezing my child
We are in Augsburg tomorrow
Augsburg tomorrow
You must do your exercises
do you understand
the exercises
Come here
do your exercises
then you'll be warm

Juggler *(who has not yet found the rosin)*:
Your grandfather means you
well

    Granddaughter *stations herself in front of* **Caribaldi** *and does an exercise at his command which consists of her standing first on the right, then on the left leg, on tiptoe, when she stands on the right leg she raises the left arm and leg and so on, when she raises the right, she drops the left arm and leg and vice versa, exactly like a puppet, with ever-increasing rapidity, while the* **Juggler** *watches from the floor.*

    Caribaldi *beating time with the bow of his cello.*

Caribaldi: Onetwo
onetwo
onetwo
onetwo
onetwo
onetwo
onetwo
onetwo
onetwo
onetwo
onetwo
onetwo
onetwo
onetwo
onetwo
onetwo
onetwo
onetwo
now stop

    Granddaughter *stops, exhausted;* **Caribaldi** *commands*
Peel apples
Clean shoes
Scald milk
Brush clothes
And be punctual for the rehearsal
you understand
You can go
    Exit **Granddaughter;** **Caribaldi** *thoughtfully*
Augsburg tomorrow
    To the **Juggler.**
Have you found the rosin
    Juggler *has not found the rosin, and carries on looking.*
A beautiful child
worthless
    Because he knows himself unobserved, pulls up his right trouser-leg still further and, while the **Juggler** *is still looking for the rosin, plays his wooden leg with the bow of the cello, slowly, as if with great relish, saying*
Casals
Casals
    Juggler *has found the rosin;* **Caribaldi** *drops his right trouser-leg;* **Juggler** *stands up with the rosin;* **Caribaldi** *with embarrassment*
Everything is music
everything
The world is
the macroanthropos
    Juggler *brings* **Caribaldi** *the rosin;* **Caribaldi** *takes the rosin and rubs the bow with it, looking at the* **Juggler.**
Experience shows
that if one
crawls about for some time
on the dirty floor
one gets dirty
    Pokes the **Juggler** *in the stomach with the bow.*
It is fear
nothing but fear
    Plays three low notes, calm and speculative, on the cello,

suddenly vehement.
A letter
even if it is from Sarrasani
gets you all worked up
   Suddenly vigorous and menacing.
But I know all about that
Every year
you receive several
such letters
all these letters
offers
higher offers
   Plucks the cello several times.
I understand
More money
More esteem
Mr Juggler
is yet again demanding more money
and more esteem
   Plucks the cello.
Two are
separated by the third
and united
Juggler: But
Caribaldi: Keep quiet
It is always the same
When people have made a name for themselves
they demand money
and esteem
more and more money
and more and more esteem
Artists blackmail with their art
if that is not real perfidy
All of a sudden artists assail you
with their demands
   Plucks the cello briefly twice.
Even genius
is reduced to megalomania
where money is concerned

Pokes the **Juggler** *in the stomach with his bow.*
Esteem
Bursts out laughing but breaks off again immediately.
Performers
in fact all artists
blackmail with their art
in the most ruthless fashion
But that does not impress me
And your letter from Sarrasani
is one of those hundreds of forged letters
you have continually held under my nose
throughout the ten or eleven years
you have been with me
Show me the offer
Show me the offer
   Plucks the strings briefly a few times and grips the bow as if he is about to play. **Juggler** *takes a step back, then another.*
He's a fool
who still believes an artist these days
a fool.

CURTAIN

SCENE TWO

Lion-Tamer *at the open piano with his left arm heavily bandaged eating bread, sausage and radish.*

Clown *(on the floor right,*
to the **Lion-Tamer***)*:
  Painful
Lion-Tamer: Not to speak of
Clown: Is the rehearsal on
Lion-Tamer: Perhaps
  perhaps not
  Thumps his bandaged hand on the keys.
Clown: That's no good
Lion-Tamer: That's no good
  no good like that
  Thumps on the keys again with his bandaged hand.
  No good
Clown: No good
  Loses his hat, puts it back on again immediately.
  What will happen now
  if we can't rehearse today
Lion-Tamer: The quintet
  can't be played
  if I can't play
Clown: If you can't play
  no
Lion-Tamer: No
  Not at all
  it's a quintet
  you see

33

Clown: Will you take me for a walk
   tomorrow
Lion-Tamer: In Augsburg tomorrow
   yes
   Then I'll take you for a walk
Clown: It must hurt
   He bit
   really hard
Lion-Tamer: really hard
   really hard
Clown: It is not my fault
   I
Lion-Tamer: All right
   that'll do
Clown: I jump
Lion-Tamer: You jump
Clown: Then he jumps too
Lion-Tamer: Max
   Looks at his bandaged hand.
   Max
   bites
   deep
Clown: It's not my fault
   I jump
   Jumps up.
   you see
   like this
   Demonstrates how he jumped in the ring.
   like this
   you see
   And he jumps too
Lion-Tamer: Max must not be irritated
   you see
   Max cannot take
   a joke
   You must keep exactly to what we agreed
   You only jump
   when I give you the sign
   with my thumb you see

You jumped too early
jumped too early
When I say Max
Max three times
Max rapidly three times
you jump
as arranged
he must jump at you
not me
You provoke him
you provoke
the animal
I can't do
the somersault
you see

    Clown *does a somersault and crouches on the floor again.*

Max cannot take
a joke

    Clown *stands up and shows the* **Lion-Tamer** *how he must provoke the lion and do a somersault when Max jumps.*

That's it
you see
that's it
We've done the act for two years

    Throws the **Clown** *a piece of sausage that he has just cut off, the* **Clown** *catches it and gobbles it up.*

There's a mistake time and time again

    Yells at the **Clown**.

No more mistakes
you understand
no more mistakes
The next time he will tear
my whole arm off
Be precise
As my uncle always says
Be precise
Make a habit of precision
you understand

    Throws the **Clown** *a big piece of sausage as if the* **Clown**

was a wild animal
Egghead
The effort
the two-and-a-half spring jump
has cost me alone
a year
you know
Now he has mastered
the jump
   From now on continually drinks beer from bottles the **Clown** *puts on the piano for him.*
You must never let him
out of your sight
Tomorrow in Augsburg
new bandages
you understand
Say Max
say quietly Max
and don't let him out of your sight
Hypnosis
you understand
My uncle
has no time
for hypnosis
The animals obey me
conversely
I obey the animals
you understand
Hypnosis
   Suddenly.
In an emergency
throw yourself flat
You must have learnt that in the Italian troupe
how you throw yourself flat
   Clown *throws himself flat as in the Italian troupe, stands up again.*
That's it
that's how it's done
Idiotic

a conspiracy
with the animals on the one hand
against the animals
on the other hand
Clown: On the one hand
on the other hand
Lion-Tamer: First comes fear
then the taste
for fear
my uncle says
Clown: The boss
Mr Caribaldi
Lion-Tamer: The boss

Lion-Tamer has knocked the bottle of beer off the piano, accidentally or not, Clown jumps up and mops up the beer with a rag.

Classical music
is killing me
Clown: The Trout quintet
Lion-Tamer: The whole of classical music

After he has wiped the beer from the floor the Clown puts a new bottle of beer on the piano for the Lion-Tamer and crouches down on the floor again where he was crouched before. Lion-Tamer drinks.

You should have seen
his daughter
a beauty
she was completely mutilated
her father had
made her do
the exercise of how to curtsy
fourteen times
just as he also makes
his granddaughter
do this exercise
fourteen times
She made a mistake
you see
Her collar bone

    was sticking in her temple
        Demonstrates.
Clown *(imitates him)*:
    In her temple
Lion-Tamer: Third class burial
    her father loves his daughter so much
    she's just bundled into the grave
    and a year later
    nobody knew any longer
    where
    he couldn't find her
    in the cemetery
    Since then he no longer goes
    to Osnabruck
    Osnabruck no longer
Clown: No longer Osnabruck
Lion-Tamer: His own daughter
    bundled into the grave
    like a dog
    you understand
    The highest degrees of difficulty
    and always ruthless
    always the same exercises
    always the same ruthlessness
    He knows no weariness
    He knows no let-up
    No dissent of any sort
    Once a year
    a new costume
    or a pair of rubber boots
    nothing else
    He calls them
    simple creatures
    my uncle
    is the genius
    who makes the creatures dance
    or train
    or juggle
    who looks up from below

he's the genius
you understand
   Cuts off a piece of sausage and throws it to the **Clown** *who catches it and gobbles it up.*
If the child takes longer than usual dressing
   Clown's *hat falls off and he puts it back on again immediately.*
she gets a smack
and her exercises are doubled
as punishment
How to curtsy
you understand
These exercises
onetwo
onetwo
onetwo
you understand
and to have to get up suddenly in the night
and do the exercise
How to curtsy
   Cuts off a piece of radish and throws it to the **Clown**.
Here's radish
radish here
   Clown *catches the piece of radish and swallows it.*
No sympathy
if her night-dress is damp
But one time such a creature
will throw herself away
and plunge
into the ring
The madness
of a single man
into which this man ruthlessly
drags everyone else
Who has nothing but destruction
in his head
   Clown's *hat falls off and he puts it on again immediately.*
To do her exercises in the rain
three degrees above zero

How to curtsy
The cello
and the whip
you understand
> *Cuts off a piece of radish and throws it to the* **Clown**, *who catches it and eats it.*

He says
I am stupid
in front of everybody

Clown: Perform your tricks
perform your tricks
Practise
practise
practise
> *Does one somersault forwards and one somersault back.*

Lion-Tamer: I hate him for that
> *Cuts off a piece of sausage and throws it to the* **Clown**.

Contempt for everything
you understand
His opponent
always
in every case an idiot
He was in Venice
with his granddaughter
They went to every thing
Even in St Mark's Square
in the rain
at two degrees Centigrade
she had to practise
How to curtsy
> *Drinks, eats.*

When you look at Max
you must think hypnosis
it is a question
of hypnosis
If you forget that
he will tear a piece
out of you
like he did me

Clown: Does it hurt
Lion-Tamer: Not
  with schnaps
  first schnaps
  then beer
  beer
  beer
Clown: With schnaps
  with beer
  with beer
  beer
  beer
Lion-Tamer: Hypnosis
  you understand
  That time
  I was lucky
  dead lucky
  But do you think
  he dropped
  my animal act
    Exclaims.
  A piece torn out of me
  and my animal act
  still goes on
  you understand
  He is always
  hounding us
  always two steps behind us
  or he's already standing in front of us
  even when he isn't there
  he is there
  he watches us
  you know
  spies on us
  Kill him with his own wooden leg
  like a dog
Clown (*his hat falls off and he puts it on again immediately*):
  Like a dog
Lion-Tamer: Like a dog

But always punctual
for the Trout quintet
> *Lifts his bandaged arm.*

Here under the shoulder
it shoots up
a shooting pain
> *Drinks.*

And I am gradually losing
my sight
the doctor predicted I would
Clown: Your sight
Lion-Tamer: In Augsburg tomorrow
I must consult the oculist
Clown: In Augsburg tomorrow
Lion-Tamer:
> *Completely empties the bottle,* **Clown** *jumps up and puts a new bottle on the piano and crouches on the floor again.*

To keep a man
like an animal
you understand
We are nothing
but animals
The piano
the viola
the bass
the violin
Animals
nothing but animals
Clown: Animals
Lion-Tamer: He drops the rosin
on purpose
Lately even
in front of the juggler
The juggler has to get down on the floor
> *Points under the chest.*

There under the chest
> *Cuts off a piece of sausage and throws it to the* **Clown.**

Mister Juggler crawls about on the floor
and retrieves the rosin for my uncle

Clown: Mister Juggler
and Mister Caribaldi
Lion-Tamer: More and more frequently
you understand
Retrieves
Sometimes I think
go on bite
But he doesn't
I dream
he has bitten off
my head
that he does bite
Mister Lion-Tamer
without his head
you understand
> **Clown** *laughs to himself.*

That he goes ahead
you understand
The head says Max
and is already bitten off
> **Clown** *laughs.*

My hands
on my head
but there is no head any more
> **Clown** *laughs to himself.*

He pounces on me
and bites off my head
> *Drinks from the bottle;* **Clown** *jumps up and loses his cap, puts it on again immediately, looking towards the door in alarm.*

Caribaldi *(enters, to the* **Clown***)*:
Unbelievable
Get out
Get into the ring
do your tricks
make it quick
> *Exit* **Clown** *with a bow to* **Caribaldi**.

I've been looking for him
all over the place

A monstrosity
Augsburg tomorrow
The Juggler alone
in the ring
the whole time
No trace
of the Clown
The audience don't find
it funny at all
   To the **Lion-Tamer**.
Beer
Radish
Stench
This isn't a place
for a drunkard
There is no place here
for a drunkard
stick to the rules
Lion-Tamer: But
Caribaldi: It is always the same
someone has to chase you up
   Animatedly.
Out with you
The animals are roaring with hunger
and you are stuffing your face
Get out
   Lion-Tamer *stands up. Yells at the* **Lion-Tamer**.
Lazy dog
   Exit **Lion-Tamer** *with the big radish*.
   Caribaldi *hangs his top-hat on the peg*.
Caribaldi: Hang up my hat
Hang up my hat
Music-stands
these useless music-stands
   Bangs into one of the music-stands, seizes one of the music-stands.
The Trout quintet
   Beats himself on the head. **Granddaughter** *has come in*.
Hang up my hat

hang up my hat
Granddaughter: The shoe-polish has run out
Caribaldi *(mimics her)*:
   The shoe-polish has run out
   In Augsburg tomorrow
   in Augsburg tomorrow
   These useless music-stands
   The Trout quintet
   Hang up my hat
   everything
   hang
   everything
      Slaps his brow.
   Idiot
Granddaughter: Do you want the cello
Caribaldi: The cello
   the cello
      Bellows at his **Granddaughter.**
   The Maggini
   or the Salo
   or the Ferraracello
      Sits down.
   Come here my child
      Granddaughter *goes up to him.*
   Listen
   the last phrase softly
   Crescendo
   when I say crescendo
   Decrescendo
   when I say
   decrescendo
   very softly
   the last phrase
   very very softly
      Strokes her on the temple.
   We are
   surrounded by beasts
   by beasts
   decrescendo

decrescendo
crescendo
crescendo
> *Looks towards the door.*

Just you and me
my child
Augsburg tomorrow
Do you sleep well
at night
I don't sleep
I don't dream
show me your legs
> **Granddaughter** *exhibits her legs.*

Your capital
Your mother
had the loveliest legs
Practise
most meticulously
Practise
Wake up
Get up
Practise
practise
practise
> *Plucks the cello, plays a long low note on the cello.*

Hear that
Casals
The art of dancing on the tight-rope
is a gift from God
And your teeth
Show me
> **Granddaughter** *opens her mouth and displays her teeth.*

Good teeth
the most important thing
Do the exercise
thirteen
Thirteen up
thirteen down
And the exercise

twenty-one
twenty-one up
twenty-one down
No reading
my child
And remember
ballet is something different
No ballet
And don't listen
to what the Lion-Tamer says
and don't listen
to what the Juggler says
It is a misunderstanding
you understand
all a misunderstanding
Arms up
    Granddaughter *throws up her arms.*
Up
up
    Granddaughter *throws her arms up twice.*
And keep away from the animals
    Shouts.
And keep away from the animals
Your poor mother
And then the fall
Let's see your hands
    Granddaughter *shows him her hands.*
Good
The continual warnings
of her father
of myself
useless
Rosin
you hear
Rosin
In Augsburg tomorrow
One day
she went to see the animals
and the animals bit her

bit into the poor creature
She was brave
the doctors
patched her up well
she had hardly been patched up
when she fell
Inattention
A moment of fear
you understand
A false step
Arms up
> **Granddaughter** *throws up her arms.*

Up
up
up
> **Granddaughter** *throws her arms up three times.*

No library in Augsburg
No book
nothing
> *Suddenly shouts.*

Keep away from the animals
Granddaughter: Keep away from the animals
Caribaldi: Dance on the tight-rope
high up
as high as can be
> *Looks up.*

Without falling down
It is a beautiful sight
> *Suddenly looking at the ground.*

That scream
my child
She died instantly
When you were on the tight-rope
for the first time
I was afraid
mortally afraid
> *Strokes his* **Granddaughter**.

I am always
afraid

Pushes her away. **Granddaughter** *spins round like a top.*
It is music
and the human ear
It is feats of skill
and music
Now bring me the cello
    Granddaughter *goes to chest, returns with the Maggini.*
not that cello
My child no
Not the Maggini
The Ferraracello
    Granddaughter *goes back to the chest with the Maggini, back to* **Caribaldi** *with the Ferraracello.*
One day
in public
in the ring
    Granddaughter *gives* **Caribaldi** *the rosin he rubs the bow with the rosin, gives the rosin to the* **Granddaughter** *and plays two long low notes.*
In public
Perhaps in the autumn
in Nuremberg
Granddaughter: In Nuremberg
Caribaldi: But keep it quiet
Keep it quiet
    Puts his forefinger to his mouth.
Keep it quiet
The Trout quintet
in the ring
First you dance on the tight-rope
and then you play the viola
softly
very softly
crescendo
decrescendo
Perfection
Absolute
People come
and see

and listen
   Plays a long low note on the cello.
They come
to a circus performance
and hear the Trout quintet
But until we get that far
until Nuremberg
We must practise
practise
practise
Schubert
nothing else
not the leopards
not the lions
not the horses
Just you
and Schubert
Not the act with the plates
Just Schubert
and you
Then
It is not a rehearsal
it is a concert
   With sudden vehemence.
But that man
with his continual injuries
and the Juggler
with his perversity
the dreadful personality
of the Clown
These terrible people
   Contemplating the cello.
A treasure
I bought it in Venice
with your mother's inheritance
this cello cost
me
her entire fortune
You see here

Indicating.
The word Ferrara is engraved
The sacred word
Ferrara
I have heard him twice
my child
Once in Paris
and once in London
Casals
  Plays a long low note back and forth.
There is a difference
Do you hear the difference
Can you hear the difference
I ask you every day
whether you can hear the difference
do you hear it
  Granddaughter *nods.*
It is a high art
the art of hearing
my child
The art is
to hear
and always
to hear the difference
Do you hear the difference
  Granddaughter *nods.*
Bring me the other one
  Gives his **Granddaughter** *the Ferraracello.* **Granddaughter** *goes to the chest and fetches the Maggini, gives it to* **Caribaldi** *and stands in front of him.* **Caribaldi** *plays a long soft note on the Maggini.*
Do you hear the difference
That difference
Casals
It is impossible
to play the Maggini cello
after five o'clock in the afternoon
The Maggini in the morning
the Ferrara in the evening

We are
north of the Alps my child
Waiting for an answer.
And
Granddaughter: We are north of the Alps
Caribaldi: Correct
we are north of the Alps
Not the Maggini
north of the Alps
not the Maggini
With sudden urgency.
The rehearsal will take place
Even if I have to kick them all
to their instruments
Mister Lion-Tamer thinks
he can allow himself an injury day in day out
and the Clown complains
of pains in his kidneys
and Mister Juggler
has been pleading
an indefinable illness for years
The rehearsal will take place
If you don't rehearse you achieve nothing
if you don't practise
you are nothing
we must rehearse incessantly
incessantly
you understand
incessantly on the tight-rope
incessantly on the viola
incessantly
we must not cease
we must not pause
Plays a long low note on the cello.
A morning instrument
not an evening instrument
not an evening instrument
Gives the Maggini to his **Granddaughter,** *who puts it in the chest and comes back with the Ferraracello,* **Caribaldi**

takes the Ferraracello and plays a long low note.
You hear
that's it
Yes
that's it
   Suddenly in a loud voice, intimidating his **Granddaughter**.
Crescendo
when I say crescendo
Decrescendo
when I say decrescendo
Is that understood
there is no excuse for negligence
Casals
   Plucks at a string.
This art
is a mathematical art
my dear child
Give me your hand
   Granddaughter *gives* **Caribaldi** *her hand.*
But you are freezing
my child
   Granddaughter *takes a step back, lifts his bow, prods his* **Granddaughter** *with the bow, beating time for her as she meekly begins her exercises.*
Caribaldi: Onetwo
   onetwo
   onetwo
   onetwo
   onetwo
   onetwo
   onetwo
   onetwo
   onetwo
   onetwo
   onetwo
   onetwo
   onetwo
      Granddaughter *exhausted, drops her arms and head.*

Now you are warm
my child
And
How do we curtsy
    Granddaughter *curtsies.*
That's how we curtsy
that's it
    Scrutinizes his **Granddaughter***'s face.*
You have no control over your face
my child
You must control your face
in Augsburg tomorrow
    Plays a long low note on the cello.
This tone
is quite different
do you hear this tone
do you hear the difference
The Ferraracello
    Granddaughter *nods.*
The heavenly bodies
are fossils
    Plays a long soft note. **Juggler** *enters,* **Caribaldi** *does not notice;* **Juggler** *and* **Granddaughter** *listen to* **Caribaldi***'s long note; when the note has ceased*
Even one misfortune
creates a pattern for the rest of your life
A Caribaldi
not an artist
Inconceivable
    Points upwards with his bow.
It is a question of air strata
    Notices the **Juggler***.*
you understand
a question of air strata
Metaphysics perhaps
Fixed and fluid
polar opposites
United
in the notion

of fire
    Suddenly.
How far
have they got
Everything must be speeded up
Tomorrow at six
I want to be in Augsburg
As soon as the performance starts
Dismantling the tent
The audience is still sitting there
but the tent is no longer there
Get on get on
get on straight away
How many were there then
Nothing more depressing
than the last performance
I hate
I can't see anything
I only smell
that unpleasant odour
given off by the audience
It is ridiculous
to keep on about this all the time
but the smell of the audience
is disgusting
I can't see anything
that is true
but I can smell
where I am
Such and such a smell I think
Ah Koblenz
Such and such a smell
Ah Berlin
such and such a smell
Nuremberg etcetera
I smell where I am
    Shouts.
Augsburg is
the worst

Cut short
the act with the animals
cut short
the act with the plates
cut down on the pranks
of the Clown
you understand
Buy fresh meat
in Augsburg
If only it was as easy as that
with fresh meat
Everybody at five in the morning
to the cheap-meat department
    To his **Granddaughter**.
You too my child
and put on your shawl
The cheap-meat department
Fresh meat
did you hear
Fresh meat
    To the **Juggler**
No cuts
in the children's show
More of the Clown
the Clown over and over again
No big words
Mister Juggler sir
And *all* the animals
All the animals
It is disgusting
my entire childhood
a reign of terror
    Drops his bow and the **Juggler** *and the* **Granddaughter** *rush over to pick up the bow, the* **Juggler** *picks it up and gives it to* **Caribaldi**.
Caribaldi: We must not forget the misery
that was our childhood
Every childhood
    To his **Granddaughter**.

Mind your back
when you bend down
you bend down too casually
unconscious
yet conscious
understand
    To the **Juggler**.
I am always telling her the same thing
just as I am always telling everybody
the same thing
none of these people change
but it is impossible
to stop giving
these admonitions
About bodies
as well as heads
About bodies and heads
Everything under constant
instant control
    To his **Granddaughter**.
How do we curtsy
    Granddaughter *immediately takes up her position*.
Well
    Granddaughter *curtsies*.
That's it
that's the way
    To the **Juggler**.
Do you think
my granddaughter
curtsies correctly
Juggler: She curtsies
correctly
Mr
Caribaldi
Caribaldi: Head and body
  bodies and heads
  under constant control
  Thoughtlessness
  is the most disgusting thing

Juggler *goes over to a picture hanging opposite him in order to put it straight;* **Caribaldi** *with regard to this picture:*
Verona
as you see
Saint Zeno
My father dying
on that miserable bedstead
you know
in an unheated room
stone floor
The sheet
for a shroud
fatal
you understand
all fatal
There on that stone floor
my dying father had
his bed
My mother
who knows where she was
Then my father said
on his death-bed
Never let it
come to this
in your life
  Lowers his bow to the **Juggler**.
Another nail
another nail is what it wants
You no sooner put it straight
than it's crooked again
Juggler: Another nail
Caribaldi: It is still not straight
  Juggler *thinks the picture is straight, but* **Caribaldi** *says:*
It is still not straight
still not
still not
still not
not quite
there

Ah
You shouldn't have touched the picture again
    Juggler *adjusts it again.*
No
no
no
Yes there
there
    Juggler *steps back and regards the picture;* **Granddaughter** *has placed herself exactly between* **Caribaldi** *and the picture;* **Caribaldi** *as if he wanted to drive her away with his bow.*
Out of the way
out of the way my
That's it
now it's straight
    To the **Juggler.**
You shouldn't have touched the picture again
It doesn't irritate me
It irritates you
You are afflicted by it
I am not afflicted by it
Bright shining mirrors
you love that
Your shoes highly polished
    Juggler, Caribaldi *and* **Granddaughter** *look at the* **Juggler***'s highly polished shoes.*
I know
you always have
a shoe-cloth
in your trousers
in your trousers on the right
A shoe-cloth on the right
a handkerchief on the left
Shoe-cloth
Handkerchief
Shoe-cloth
Handkerchief
    Commanding to **Juggler.**
Show us then

show us
> *Indicates to the* **Juggler** *with his bow to turn out his trouser-pockets.*

Turn out
your pockets
Turn them out
> **Juggler** *turns out his pockets, but the shoe-cloth appears on the left and the handkerchief on the right, not the other way round.*

You see
You haven't got the handkerchief
in your left hand pocket
but in the right
You have the shoe-cloth in the left
Even you make mistakes
Mr Juggler
Put it all back again
> **Juggler** *pockets shoe-cloth and handkerchief again, but this time properly, the shoe-cloth in the right pocket, the handkerchief in the left.*

Pocket-jugglery
pocket jugglery
> *To his* **Granddaughter**.

a self-respecting person
has a shoe-cloth in his right-hand pocket
and a handkerchief
in his left-hand pocket
And he does not confuse
left and right-hand pockets
And he has a cleaner
white handkerchief
> *To the* **Juggler**.

I will not ask you
how many clean white handkerchiefs
you possess
> *To his* **Granddaughter**.

He washes his handkerchiefs
himself
he is unmarried

he washes them himself
in a special basin
Because it would not do
for him to wash his face
in the same basin
in which he washes his handkerchiefs
and his shoe-cloths
Even shoe-cloths must be washed
now and again my child
    To the **Juggler**.
One time in Iserlohn
you blew your nose
in the shoe-cloth
and wiped your nose
with the shoe-cloth
Do you remember
that terrible
persistent cold you had
    Granddaughter *suddenly bursts out laughing.* **Caribaldi** *spitefully.*
In Iserlohn
And in Marburg on the Lahn
    Glancing at his **Granddaughter**.
In front of the audience
too
    Lion-Tamer *enters, all look at the* **Lion-Tamer** *who stops in the doorway;* **Caribaldi** *yelling at the Lion-Tamer*
Fresh meat
in Augsburg tomorrow
Fresh meat
    To himself and to his **Granddaughter**.
What a repulsive man
    Lion-Tamer *goes to the piano and collects a big radish and is about to go, but the* **Clown** *comes in;* **Granddaughter** *looks at the* **Clown**: **Caribaldi** *puts his ear to the cello and plays a long low note, three times back and forth;* **Clown** *beckons* **Granddaughter** *to him and whispers something in her ear and points under the chest with outstretched hand;* **Granddaughter** *goes to the chest and takes out the rosin and*

goes with it to **Caribaldi**.
 Caribaldi *has not noticed his* **Granddaughter** *at first, plays a long low note, breaks off and takes the rosin from her and rubs the bow of the cello with it—suddenly to the* **Clown**
Have you done your act
 Clown *nods;* **Caribaldi** *to his* **Granddaughter**
How do we curtsy
 Granddaughter *curtsies.*

CURTAIN

SCENE THREE

Everyone apart from the **Lion-Tamer** *on the chairs tuning their instruments, rubbing the bows with rosin.*

Caribaldi: *(to his* **Granddaughter***):*
Crescendo
when I say crescendo
Decrescendo
when I say decrescendo
There are no excuses
in art
even in circus tricks
   To the **Juggler**.
This development
must be pursued alone
making genius
of imbecility
in a single moment
When a body as a whole
enters a relationship
then its parts enter
into a similar relationship
as the whole body
The hundreds and thousands of directions
in which I could have gone
I went in only one
But I am not a good example
in fact I have
failed

The ringmaster has always
failed
The attempts
I have made
failed
the possibilities
I have had
Because a man like me
is bound to destroy himself
in the continual observation
of other people
To let others develop by themselves
is forbidden a man
like me
In itself a mediocre affinity
and High Art
on the other hand
And the continual attempts
to grind
the mediocrity of this affinity
down into
this High Art
or rather this so-called High Art
This quintet rehearsal day in day out
is more than just a whim
    To his **Granddaughter**.
Play the viola
the way you dance on the tight-rope
    To the **Juggler**.
Make the violin
the head of the whole ensemble
and vice versa
you know
    To the **Clown**.
The bass
is your misfortune
you understand
again and again
The bass

is your misfortune
Always these delays
these injuries
these moods
>   *To his* **Granddaughter**.

Don't forget the E-string
in Augsburg
A completely crazy music-dealer
in Augsburg
It is always the Lion-Tamer
who sabotages the quintet
>   *Yells.*

Sabotage
Sabotage

Juggler: His wound is festering
the Lion-Tamer says
with a festering wound

Caribaldi: His wound is festering
his wound is festering
with a festering wound
But it is a quintet
not a quartet
And because he continually
has festering wounds
he gets drunk
and then it is impossible for him
to find his way about on the piano
He cannot find his way about on the piano
>   *Plays a long low note on the cello;* **Juggler** *plays a note on the violin;* **Granddaughter** *plucks the viola;* **Clown** *plucks the bass.*

Casals
>   *Plays a low long note on the cello.*

Casals
>   *To the* **Juggler**.

Do you hear the difference
>   *Plays a low long note on the cello.*

Casals
>   *Suddenly commanding.*

The tuning note please
ALL play a long note on their instruments.
We might now manage
what we have not managed
for ages
but the Lion-Tamer
destroys everything
Arranges the music on the music-stand.
Radish
the stench of radish everywhere
Juggler *blows the dust off his music.*
Ruthlessness
is an artistic resolve
the only possibility
lies in ruthlessness
But the world around us
is nothing but stupidity
and disease
and incomprehension
I have been playing the cello for decades
in a fight against dull-headedness
But there is no end in sight
no end in sight
Plucks the cello.
Perfection
Society kicks
out
anyone who kicks against it
To his **Granddaughter**.
You must play the viola
the way you dance on the tight-rope
you understand
Two strings in Augsburg
E E you understand
E-strings
To the **Juggler**.
All your life
my dear Mr Juggler
all your life

You'll also be juggling with your plates
all your life
against society
Your head will find no peace
against society
    To the **Clown**.
Melancholic
    Clown *plays three short notes back and forth on the bass.*
With the bow
with the violin-bow
with the bass-bow
with the cello-bow
against everything
One's head is no longer
left in peace by the art
one produces
if it stops
it is dead
to play oneself
into death
with the bow
    Plays a long low note on the cello; of the **Lion-Tamer** *to the* **Clown**.
The way he throws you
the pieces of sausage
and the pieces of radish
    Plays a long low note on the cello; **Granddaughter** *picks her nose;* **Caribaldi** *has noticed this; to the* **Juggler**.
You haven't managed to cure
my granddaughter
of picking her nose
she's hardly sat down on the chair
and she's picking her nose
    To his **Granddaughter**.
That is a nasty habit
my child
even while you are playing
you pick your nose
It is repulsive

67

to pick your nose
during the Trout quintet
  To the **Juggler**.
Or that terrible habit
of coughing in the middle of the andante
such a distinguished
well-trained fellow
and such a terrible habit
You must eat more malt
a lot more malt
you understand
And if you really do
the breathing exercises
I recommended
Out at six in the morning
makes no difference where
even in Augsburg
an hour or even only
half an hour
in the fresh air
with the crescendo in mind
you understand
This contraction of your afflicted bronchia
You will clear them
You will be free of all complaints
in no time at all
But you ignore
what I say
That's why you also have problems
with the eighteenth plate
you can't do it
Because you have difficulties
with your breathing
breathing difficulties
  To all of them.
You all have breathing difficulties
Your breathing doesn't function
that's what it is
If your breathing functions

High Art functions too
For an artist
for a practising artist
especially for an artiste
or for someone
who is both performing practising artist
and artiste
performing artiste
control of your breathing
is the most important thing
> *Directly to the* **Juggler**.

Your language is also
composed only of the shortest sentences
your speech consists
only of the shortest sentences
whereas orderly long
long orderly sentences
would suit your overall image
What you say
is disjointed
everything you say
is disjointed
That indicates
you have no control
over your breathing
that is a disgrace
for a performer
> *To all of them.*

I have been working
all my life
To get rid of
the interferences
infirmities of the organism
> *All play a note on their instruments together upon* **Caribaldi**'s *silent command.*

There
that's good
But the piano has let us down
once again

  Juggler *coughs*.
We have hardly played a couple of bars
and you break in with your cough
  Clown's *hat falls over his eyes*.
Or the Clown's hat falls
off his head
His hat is constantly
slipping off his head
  Directly to the **Clown**.
Haven't you got a hat
that isn't continually
slipping down then
he has hardly sat down
and his hat slips off
  Granddaughter *laughs*. **Caribaldi** *to the* **Juggler**.
Of course she would laugh at that
  Yells at his **Granddaughter**.
Go on laugh
  To the **Juggler**.
My granddaughter's
dreadful laughter
when the Clown's hat
slips off
If the hat is too big for him
it slips off
if it's too small for him
it slips off
Then he can't see anything
and there's a wrong note
immediately there's a wrong note
if there's a wrong note
I know
his hat has fallen down
  To the **Juggler**.
Isn't there any way
of stopping his hat slipping off
Screw it on to his head
But we can't
screw it on to his head

on to his head
> **Clown**'s *hat slips over his eyes;* **Granddaughter** *laughs.*

There goes the hat
> **Clown** *puts his hat back on again;* **Granddaughter** *laughs.*

The hat falls down
and my granddaughter laughs
My granddaughter laughs
when the hat falls down

Juggler: First the hat
falls down

Caribaldi: Then my granddaughter
laughs
> **Clown** *bursts out laughing.*

The Clown
must not laugh
he has nothing
to laugh about

Clown *(stops laughing, says)*:
Nothing to laugh about
nothing to laugh about

Juggler *(points the bow of his violin at him)*:
The Clown
must not laugh
He has nothing to laugh about

Caribaldi: Not the Clown
> *To his* **Granddaughter**.

You will pay
dearly
for that laughter
Four days of potato soup
that will get rid of
your laughter
> *Plays a note on the cello, then*

Or I have this
terrible rheumatic pain
I got
on the Stilfser pass
You remember
on the Stilfser pass

Juggler: On the Stilfser pass
Granddaughter ⎫
Clown ⎭ *(together):*
 On the Stilfser pass
Caribaldi: A draught
 Just a draught
Clown: A draught
 Drops his hat and puts it back on immediately.
Caribaldi *(yells at the* **Clown***):*
 A draught
 To the **Juggler***.*
 This terrible pain in my back
 But I do not lose my self-control
 I do not permit myself
 pain
 while I am playing
 Plays a long low note on the cello, listens.
 The temperature is falling
 To the **Juggler***.*
 Do you hear
 the temperature is falling
 I can tell from the tone of the cello
 that the temperature is falling
 In Augsburg tomorrow
 To his **Granddaughter***.*
 Don't forget
 the hot-water bottle
 in Augsburg tomorrow
 Plays a low note on the cello.
 Augsburg
 is cold
Juggler: No greater pleasure
 than conquering pain
 with the quintet
  Granddaughter *stifles a laugh;* **Clown***'s hat falls over his eyes; to* **Caribaldi.**
 He would not be the Clown
 if from time to time
 his hat

didn't
Caribaldi: It is an impertinence
to let his hat fall down
Juggler: A sharp movement of the head
and the hat falls down
Caribaldi *(points at the head of the* **Clown** *with his bow)*:
And the hat falls down
down falls the hat
    Clown *holds the hat on his head with both hands;* **Granddaughter** *and* **Juggler** *burst out laughing.*
An impertinence
an impertinence
Juggler *(to* **Caribaldi***)*:
An awkward situation
Caribaldi: An impertinence
Juggler: An impudence
Caribaldi *(to the* **Juggler***)*: To see you laughing
Not only to hear you
laughing
To see you laughing
because of this disgusting display
    Juggler *now laughs completely openly out loud.*
There is nothing more disgusting
than the unmotivated laughter
of an intelligent man
    Clown's *hat falls over his eyes, he puts it back on again immediately and holds it on to his head with both hands. They all laugh out loud apart from* **Caribaldi**, *abruptly stop laughing;* **Caribaldi** *is about to jump up but is held back by the violent pain in his back, sits down again.*
Juggler: You must not jump up
abruptly
You know
you must not
jump up abruptly
Caribaldi: In Augsburg tomorrow
    Clutches his back.
In Augsburg tomorrow
My whole life

is a torment
all my ideas
are ruined
As if that's not enough
I am also
continually derided
> *Looking at the* **Juggler**.

disavowed
> *Looking at the* **Clown**.

duped
> *Looking at his* **Granddaughter**.

laughed at
> *To the* **Clown**.

You are driving me mad
holding your hat
on your head
with both hands
> **Clown** *takes his hands away from his head, his hat falls down;* **Caribaldi** *exclaims.*

A nightmare
a nightmare
> **Clown** *puts his hat back on again;* **Caribaldi** *looks at the clock.*

One day
I will kill
that man
That nephew of mine
> *Plays a long note on the cello and plucks at a string.*

Although he knows
we are waiting for him
he doesn't come
It is his triumph
> *Plays seven short vigorous notes on the cello.*

It is his triumph
> *Plays a short low note, breaks off.*

Casals
We must bear the shifts in temperature
in mind
> *To his* **Granddaughter**.

74

Make the shifts in temperature
our first priority
> *To the* **Jugger**.

It is a quintet
not a quartet
It is not called
Trout quartet
it is called
Trout quintet
The ones that die
> *About the* **Lion-Tamer**.

he feeds to the others
> *Plucks the cello.*

That man is always lolling about
guzzling swilling
> *Cries out.*

A destroyer
I have been punished enough
> **Caribaldi** *signals to the* **Clown** *to come right up to him;* **Clown** *goes right up to* **Caribaldi**. **Caribaldi**, *examining the* **Clown**'s *hat, to the* **Juggler**.

Perhaps it is
only a question
of the material
> *Taps the* **Clown** *on the head, asks him*

What sort of material is that

Clown: Silk
It's silk

Caribaldi *(to the* **Juggler***)*:
Silk
It's silk
it is silk
> *Cries out*

Silk silk
> *To the* **Juggler**.

Must it be silk
It must not be silk
It does not have to be silk
Linen

Linen
starched linen
 Juggler *shrugs his shoulders, to his* **Granddaughter**
It doesn't have to be silk
my child
Linen
starched linen
Granddaughter: Starched linen
Caribaldi *(to the* **Clown***):*
Give it to me
show it to me
give it to me
 Clown *gives the hat to* **Caribaldi**, **Caribaldi** *inspects the hat.*
Silk
silk
The hat is much too baggy
a much too baggy hat
Linen
linen
starched linen
I can imagine
that a linen hat
of starched linen
would stay on your head
 Seizes the head of the **Clown**.
Stays on this head
on the head
the hat
there on the head
of starched linen
 Gives the **Clown** *his hat back.* **Clown** *puts it on.*
A linen hat of course
 Clown *backing away*
A linen hat
a starched linen hat
 Clown *sits down.*
In Augsburg tomorrow
Tomorrow in Augsburg

Linen
starched linen
 To his **Granddaughter**
The hat starched
In Augsburg tomorrow
my child
In Augsburg
 Clown *loses his hat,* **Caribaldi** *yells*
Put it on
put on your hat
put on your hat
 Clown *puts on the hat;* **Caribaldi** *to the* **Juggler**
A madness
a whim
a virus
Juggler *(repeats)*:
A virus
Caribaldi: A virus
 Clutches his back.
Everything is against
the rehearsal
against me
 Cries out
You are all against me
I ought to send you all to the devil
 Clutches his hip.
The further north
the greater the pain
 To the **Juggler**
Is there a doctor
in Augsburg
a rheumatism specialist
in that detestable muggy hole
In that sewer of the Lech
 To his **Granddaughter**
You still have to rub my back today
my child
from the bottom to the top
you understand

slowly from the bottom
to the top
Get the juices flowing
the juices flowing
Juggler *(to the* **Granddaughter***)*:
The painful juices in the back
need to be well
shaken
Caribaldi: Shake
shake
you understand
Juggler *(to* **Caribaldi***)*:
These rheumatic juices
must be well shaken
Caribaldi *(to the* **Juggler***)*:
Or perhaps I will have
my nephew rub my back
those great those enormous thumbs
of my nephew do me good
   To his **Granddaughter**
Your hands are
chicken bones
like chicken bones
no
   To the **Juggler**
Those enormous thumbs
of my nephew you know
   Clown *now plays several long low notes on the bass;*
Caribaldi *to the* **Juggler**
My nephew
is all right
for rubbing my back
otherwise he is
good for nothing
   Granddaughter *plays several notes on the viola while the*
Clown *does the same on the bass;* **Caribaldi** *to the* **Juggler**
Those great fleshy thumbs
you know
This ill-bred man

who has the habit
of constantly eating
enormous the very biggest radishes
at the piano
at the open piano what's more
    Juggler *plays several notes on the violin, while the* **Clown** *and the* **Granddaughter** *are still playing their instruments;* **Caribaldi** *suddenly*
But this is intolerable
this out of tune piano
and this appalling stench
of radish
    All stop playing their instruments.
String instruments
string instruments
    Exclaims
Is there a piano tuner
anywhere
in Augsburg
To put such a thoroughly
unmusical man
on the piano
because one is forced to do so
    To the **Juggler**
The piano as a beer table
as a table for the consumption
the endless consumption
of radishes
    Plays a long low note on the cello, to the **Juggler**
Only genius is
the true experimenter
That is a dangerous habit
    Plays a long low note on the cello.
There is always this dreadful
this ghastly stench of radishes
in the air
Everything stinks of radishes
Juggler: Of radishes
Clown & Granddaughter: Of radishes

Caribaldi *plays a low note on the cello.*
Caribaldi: He is an animal
an illegitimate animal
Because he is a relation
A good indication
spoonfed
brought
from prison
and spoon-fed
  To the **Juggler**
His first thought was
to get hold of
some radishes
Juggler: These vast quantities
of radish
he consumes
Caribaldi: Radish
  Clown *and* **Granddaughter** *are playing their instruments again.*
Beerradish
Sodomy
sodomy
  To the **Juggler**
Beerradish
Sodomy
you understand
  Plays a long low note on the cello, breaking in on **Clown** *and* **Granddaughter**.
Sodomy
Sodomy
  Suddenly exclaiming, plucking the cello
Must we put up with it
and allow this man
to sabotage the rehearsal day in day out
  Clown's *hat falls down over his eyes.*
This is
insanity
  Clown *puts his hat back on again and holds it on with both hands, the bass between his knees, while the* **Juggler** *is stared*

at by the **Granddaughter**.
What are you sitting there
staring at him like that for
   To the **Juggler**
The child is
fascinated
by your personality
It is damaging her art
   To his **Granddaughter**
Staring at the Juggler
and neglecting everything else
No discipline on the tight-rope
but staring at the Juggler
the viola nothing
but staring at the Juggler
Not doing her sums
Forgetting to sew on
trouser-buttons
A bad creature
my child
In Augsburg tomorrow
I will buy you lots of ghastly literature
and you will have no more time
for the Juggler
learning everything by heart
   To the **Juggler**
And the dear Juggler
has no right
to take advantage of
the stupidity
and the foolishness of my granddaughter
    Clown *loses his hat,* **Caribaldi** *to the* **Juggler** *concerning the* **Clown**
We must sew his hat
to a cord
and pull the cord tight
under his chin
   To the **Clown**
The hat to a cord

and pull it tight under your chin
so that the hat
can't fall off any more
the hat
Juggler *(to* **Caribaldi***)*:
But Mr Caribaldi
that is precisely
what makes people laugh
his hat
falling off his head
  Clown *bursts out laughing,* **Granddaughter** *joins in.*
Caribaldi: Precisely that
of course
precisely that
 Plays a note; **Juggler** *coughs;* **Caribaldi** *to the* **Juggler**
Malt
do you hear
Malt
 Juggler *coughs.*
In Augsburg tomorrow
About the hat
Juggler *(to* **Caribaldi***)*:
A compromise
is necessary
Caribaldi: A compromise
a compromise
Juggler: What sort of compromise
 Clown *plays a note on the bass,* **Granddaughter** *plays a note on the viola,* **Clown** *and* **Granddaughter** *play several notes on their instruments.* **Juggler** *to* **Caribaldi**
It is quite simple
Caribaldi: Simple
Juggler: In the ring
if such a cord is sewn on
he must
Caribaldi: If such a cord
Juggler: If such a cord is really sewn on
Caribaldi: If such a cord
Juggler: If such a cord is really sewn on

    not pull it tight
Caribaldi: So that the hat
    Indicates the hat falling off.
    can fall off
Juggler: Right
    so that the hat
    can fall off
Clown: Can fall off
Caribaldi: Can fall off
Juggler: Can fall off
Clown: Can fall off
Juggler: But in your presence
    Mr Caribaldi
    he keeps the cord of the hat
    fastened
    pulled tight
    and fastened
Caribaldi: Fastened
Juggler *(demonstrates the process of fastening the hat and pulling the cord tight):*
    Fastened
    you see
Caribaldi: Fastened
Clown: Fastened
    Granddaughter *laughs.*
Juggler: When the Clown is performing
    his hat is
    not fastened
    when he is not performing
    when he is in your presence
    Mr Caribaldi
    he keeps it fastened
Caribaldi: Not fastened
Juggler: Fastened
Caribaldi: Not fastened
Juggler: Fastened
    fastened
Caribaldi: Fastened
Juggler: The hat is not fastened

so that it can fall off
Caribaldi: Can fall off
Clown: Can fall off
>   **Granddaughter** *laughs;* **Clown** *loses his hat and immediately puts it back on again;* **Granddaughter** *bursts out laughing.*

Caribaldi *(to the* **Clown***):*
>   Of course
>   when you are performing
>   the hat is
>   not fastened
>   when you are not performing
>   you keep it fastened
>   >   *To the* **Juggler**
>
>   He keeps it fastened
>   when we are playing the Trout quintet
>   >   *To the* **Clown**
>
>   Throughout the rehearsal
>   you keep it fastened

Juggler *(to* **Caribaldi***):*
>   You see
>   it is quite simple
>   when he is performing
>   his hat is not fastened
>   so that it can fall off
>   when he is not performing
>   he keeps it fastened

Caribaldi *(suddenly to the* **Juggler***):*
>   I cannot bear it
>   when his hat falls off his head
>   >   *To the* **Clown**
>
>   When you are performing
>   keep the hat fastened

Juggler *(breaks in):*
>   Not fastened
>   so that it falls off

Caribaldi: Fastened
so that it falls off
Juggler: Not fastened

Caribaldi: Not fastened of course
when you are not performing
you keep it fastened
   To the **Clown**
In Augsburg tomorrow
a cord
Juggler: Double for preference
Caribaldi: For preference double
make it tight
make it tight
under the chin
under the chin
   Shows how to pull a cord tight under the chin so that the hat cannot fall off.
Like that
you see
like that
tight
Juggler: Tight
very tight
Caribaldi: Tight
tight
Juggler: Tight
Caribaldi: So that the hat
cannot fall off
Juggler: Nobody will laugh
His whole act
is based on
his hat falling off
Caribaldi *(to the* **Clown***):* Based on
your hat continually
falling off
based on it
Juggler: And that now and then
he himself
falls down
tumbles to the ground
Caribaldi: Tumbles
tumbles

every now and then
Juggler: That is your own idea
Mr Caribaldi
that he loses his hat
and that every now and then
he himself falls down
Caribaldi: Falls down
loses his hat
his hat
falls down
Juggler: Alternately his hat falls
off his head
he falls down
It is your brain-wave
Mr Caribaldi
> **Granddaughter** *plays a long note on the viola.*

Caribaldi: It is my brain-wave
Juggler: The only important thing is
that the hat
Caribaldi: That the hat
Juggler: That the hat falls from his head
at the right moment
Caribaldi *(yells furiously at the* **Clown***)*:
That is important
did you hear
> *Threatens him with the bow.*

did you hear
> **Clown**'s *hat falls off his head and he immediately puts it back on again and holds it tight with both hands;* **Caribaldi** *with his bow raised high in the air.*

That is important
Important
Juggler: Important
Caribaldi: Very important
Clown: Important
Caribaldi: *(puts his ear to the cello and plays a long soft note)*:
Casals
never went
back to Spain again

Looks at the **Juggler**.
Never again
you understand
never again
    Plays a long soft note on the cello, then to his **Granddaughter**
And you
have you tuned your instrument
Is it tuned
Precisely because you do not have a perfect ear
    Granddaughter *gradually tunes all the strings of her viola;*
    Caribaldi *to the* **Clown**
And you
You are messing about
and not tuning your instrument
    Yells at them all
Cacophony
    To the **Clown**
You don't tune your instrument
the same as you don't clean your teeth
    To the **Juggler**
That foul smell
when he opens his mouth
Good thing the ring
is so big
otherwise he would drive away the audience
with his foul smell
How many were there then
Many
Juggler: Two dozen
Caribaldi: To play
in front of two dozen people
Augsburg tomorrow
Augsburg tomorrow
    Clown's *hat falls off and he immediately puts it back on again;* **Caribaldi** *to the* **Juggler**
Different pranks
Different acts
Different animals

different performers
completely different performers
   Hurriedly plays a high note on the cello. **Granddaughter** *plays a low note on the viola.* **Clown** *plucks at the bass several times.* **Caribaldi** *to the* **Clown**
How often have I told you
Clean your teeth
Tune your instrument
It is all the same to me
whether you clean your teeth first
or tune your bass
Give it here
   Clown *gives* **Caribaldi** *his bass,* **Caribaldi** *takes the bass, plucks it; to the* **Juggler**
Completely out of tune
an instrument completely out of tune
   Tries to tune the bass, plucks it; to the **Juggler**
You hear
you see
you hear
   Gives the bass back to the **Clown***; to the* **Juggler**
Pursuing the idea
Diseases
cured by means of diseases
Life is intensified by means of death
Cacophony
   Juggler *plucks his violin;* **Caribaldi** *plucks his cello.*
Casals took his time
Casals
   Juggler *plucks his violin;* **Granddaughter** *plays three short rapid notes on the viola;* **Juggler** *plucks the violin.*
Your higher education
is noticeable
The academy is noticeable
   To all of them
The pre-requisite is of course
a tuned instrument
I am not prepared
to be

witness to a cacophony
I do not think
the rehearsal will take place
   of the **Lion-Tamer**
But if he should turn up
Just let him come
my nephew
the Lion-Tamer
   To his **Granddaughter**
Give it to me
   Granddaughter *gives* **Caribaldi** *the viola,* **Caribaldi** *holds up the viola.*
The viola
Viola da braccio
   Tries to tune the viola.
Juggler: It depends on the side
Caribaldi: Of course it depends
on the side
   Plucks the viola and gives it back to his **Granddaughter**.
Day in day out I am checking
your instruments
Not one of you can
tune his instrument
If only it was impossible·
for you to stick out your tongue
that is disgusting
Two boxes of rosin
in Augsburg
Juggler: Lineament
Caribaldi: Lineament
   To his **Granddaughter**
I shall go with you to the Lech
and make you
say
three hundred times
on the bridge
I must tune my viola myself
There are of course musicians
in fact even those who play in an orchestra

and some even in philharmonic orchestras
who cannot tune their instruments themselves
they imagine
they can do it
but they have no ear at all
  Granddaughter *plays several notes on the viola;* **Caribaldi** *to the* **Juggler**
Together with the feeble-mindedness
of these people
of these so-called philharmonic musicians
there is also the feebleness of their ear
whole orchestras suffer from it
  They hear the **Lion-Tamer** *approaching;* **Clown** *loses his hat and immediately puts it back on again.*
Those footsteps prove
that he is drunk
  Louder
That that man
is drunk
  Lion-Tamer *enters.*
Juggler *(to* **Caribaldi** *as the* **Lion-Tamer** *comes in)*:
No good will come of this trip
to Augsburg
Caribaldi: To Augsburg
Augsburg tomorrow
  To the **Juggler** *about the* **Lion-Tamer**, *who has stopped by the door*
A drunken nephew
who mixes up the piano
with the beer-table
  To the **Lion-tamer**
Stinking
drunk
As if there is always a radish
rotting in your mouth
  To the **Juggler**
This man only appears now
as a drunkard
He uses his injuries as an excuse
There is nothing he hates more

than the Trout quintet
He has been taken over by
brutality
> **Lion-Tamer** *takes a large radish from the piano where it has been lying all the time; goes up to* **Caribaldi** *with the radish.*
>
> **Caribaldi** *pushes the* **Lion-Tamer** *away with his bow; to the* **Juggler**

A repulsive man
in the role
of a repulsive man
> *To his* **Granddaughter**

To think we are related to the repulsive
the same kith and kin
as the repulsive
> *To the* **Juggler**

To make a man
of such a monster
let alone a performer
a musician
> *From now on all pluck more and more nervously at their instruments, or play them with the same constantly growing nervousness, above all the* **Juggler**. **Caribaldi** *looking around him*

As if the rehearsal is possible
> *Exclaims*

The rehearsal is impossible
> *Straight to the* **Lion-Tamer***'s face.*

This man
has made it impossible once again
this man over and over again
> **Lion-Tamer** *goes to the piano, sits down and thumps on the keys with his bandaged arm.*

Impudence
sits at the piano
The art-wrecker
> *To the* **Juggler**

The art-wrecker
Juggler: The art-wrecker
> **Clown***'s hat slips down over his eyes and he remains with it*

like that.
Caribaldi: The art-wrecker
    Lion-Tamer *thumps his bandaged arm on the keys.*
The art-wrecker
who wrecks art
    Exclaims
Baseness at the piano
    To the **Juggler**
Humanly possible
you see
Humanly possible
    Lion-Tamer *thumps twice with his bandaged arm on the keys; pathetically to the* **Juggler**
Decades
Centuries
are destroyed in this way
The art-wrecker
Juggler: The art-wrecker
Caribaldi: The beasts are destroying
art
you hear
art is being destroyed
    Lion-Tamer *thumps several times with his bandaged arm on the keys.*
I should have known
that we were dealing with an animal
    Lion-Tamer *thumps several times with his bandaged arm on the keys more and more violently, finally he throws his shoulder again and again against the piano.* **Granddaughter** *plays a couple of notes on the viola.* **Clown** *plucks the bass.*
Juggler: Undoubtedly
an incivility
an incivility
undoubtedly
    Lion-Tamer *pummels with both arms on the keys of the piano.*
    Clown *loses his hat and immediately puts it back on again.*
    Granddaughter *plays two notes on the viola.*
Caribaldi: The child does not understand
what we are playing

> *To the* **Juggler**
You see
my granddaughter
Juggler: A good child
> **Lion-Tamer** *pummels on the keys once more;* **Juggler** *exclaims*
A terrible scene
Mr Caribaldi
Caribaldi: A terrible scene
Juggler: The conditions
the circumstances
the conditions
like the circumstances
that is how they are
Caribaldi: In vain
once more everything in vain
> *As if he is completely exhausted, he plays a long note on the cello.* **Granddaughter** *accompanies him on the viola.* **Caribaldi** *suddenly flaring up at the* **Lion-Tamer**
Get out
get out
he must get out
> *Even more vehemently*
The animal must get out
get the animal out
> **Juggler** *stands up.*
Out
out
out with the man
take the animal out
out with the animal
> *The* **Lion-Tamer**'s *head falls on the keys, his arms fall to his sides,* **Caribaldi** *yells*
Out
out
out
> *He is about to jump up but is unable to do so, sits down again.* **Granddaughter** *plucks the viola.*
Take the animal out
out with the animal

Juggler *(taking a step back)*:
   Of course
   Mr Caribaldi

   Turns to the **Lion-Tamer**, *seizes him by the hair; turns round to the* **Clown**. **Clown** *drops his cap and puts it back on again immediately, jumps up and goes over to the* **Lion-Tamer**. **Juggler** *and* **Clown** *lift the* **Lion-Tamer** *who is completely drunk.*
   He can no longer
   stand on his feet
   Mr Caribaldi
Caribaldi *(after a pause)*:
   Out
   out
   get out
Juggler: Life consists in
   destroying questions
Caribaldi *(disgusted by the* **Lion-Tamer**, *by everything)*:
   Away
   away
   away

   Granddaughter *drops the viola; exit* **Juggler** *and* **Clown** *with the* **Lion-Tamer**. **Caribaldi**, *after a pause, to his* **Granddaughter**
   You see
   you hear
   you see

   Graddaughter *rushes terrified but without a word after the others.* **Caribaldi** *gets up slowly, laboriously and leans the cello against the wall and begins to arrange music-stands, instruments and chairs along the wall and in the corners, as if he wanted to clear everything away—all of a sudden, faster and faster, with increasing haste. Once he has cleared away all the chairs and all the music-stands, he drops into the armchair, hangs his head and says*
   Augsburg tomorrow

   He turns up the radio near to him. The Trout quintet on the radio. Five bars

END